Ray Willia

THE WIZARD OF GUZZ

1950
ANNUS MIRABILIS

WITH A FOREWORD BY
ADMIRAL SIR DEREK REFFELL RN KCB

4 Corners Publishing
Chester

ISBN 0 9545394 1 9

Printed and bound in Great Britain by
Kendall Press Ltd, Manchester

4 Corners Publishing
2A Old Wrexham Road,
Chester CH4 7HS
Telephone 01244 679471

Retail Stockists

Bookland, 12 Bridge Street, Chester CH1 1NO
Tel: 01244 347323

University Bookseller, 42 Drake Circus, Plymouth PL4 8AB
Tel: 01752 660428

Dedicated to all those senior citizens
who, when they were young men, were conscripted
to do their National Service in the early post-war years
and especially to those who served as
National Servicemen in the Royal Navy.

N°. 350/500

CONTENTS

Admiral Sir Derek Reffell

FOREWORD

By Admiral Sir Derek Reffell KCB

Ray Williams and I have at least two things in common: we both went to school in or near Chester in the 1940s, and we both served in HMS Wizard in 1950. The Royal Naval College was evacuated to Eaton Hall, near Chester, after Dartmouth was bombed in 1942 and I believe we competed at cricket with Chester City Grammar School, where Ray was educated. Later, Ray and I were on the same side in Wizard's cricket team.

Full of training but short of experience, I joined the ship several months before Ray. At that time, the war was still very much in our minds and regulars, including those who, like me, had missed wartime service, were very aware of the debt the Navy and the country owed to the Reservists and National Servicemen who had formed such a large proportion of Naval Manpower and borne so much of the strain and dangers of the war.

Nevertheless, by 1950 National Service was viewed with frustration both by those conscripted and by regulars, the former because their duties often seemed irrelevant and they wanted to get on with their civilian careers; and the latter because most National Servicemen left the ship just when they began to be really useful, being replaced by others who needed 'knocking into shape'.

In retrospect, however, it is remarkable how many look back on their National Service and reflect on what it taught them about loyalty, duty and comradeship, speculating on the possible beneficial effects for today's youth of its reintroduction. Whilst I agree that, with the war fresh in our minds, it was valuable both to those involved and to the Services, I doubt if reintroduction would now have the desirable effects imagined, nor be practical in Services with more technical equipment. Be that as it may, Ray's account of his Annus Mirabilis is an interesting story of one man's National Service, and will bring back many memories for others, and for those with whom he served, as it did for me.

INTRODUCTION

Just a few helpful words to the readers of this book. Shakespeare's play Hamlet is set in Denmark, and most of the characters are Danish but nobody would expect to learn anything useful or relevant about the Denmark of today from reading Shakespeare's play. It is similar with this book and the Royal Navy.

Although the action revolves around one of his late Majesty's destroyers, HMS Wizard, the book is only partly about the Royal Navy. There are thousands of excellent books about the Navy written by experts and by people who spent a lifetime in the Senior Service. I was a National Serviceman who did twelve months at sea, and twelve months in various camps and barracks. It would be presumptuous for me to write a book about the Royal Navy, but ex-naval personnel will enjoy reading my narrative and it will bring back many memories. It is also different from other books about the Navy as it is set entirely in peacetime – no mention of any great battles or examples of heroism. It is also written from a National Service perspective.

The book is really more about social history than naval history. It is also about a world that no longer exists, about things which are unfashionable in many quarters today – discipline and punishment, courtesy and respect, determination and effort, hardship and discomfort, patriotism and duty. This book should therefore appeal to Middle England; perhaps it's the book they've been waiting for! The people who pay their rates and their taxes, who believe in a fair day's work for a fair day's pay.

Nostalgia is a complaint that no one minds having. Memory Lane is a place that those of a certain age all want to go to. But the book has not been written for the older generation. I hope that it will be of interest and possibly be an inspiration to teenagers and twenty year olds because it is about growing up, opportunity, freedom, pleasure and enjoyment. Embedded in the naval framework there is interwoven a lot about the theatre, music (especially opera), youth hostelling, hiking and hitchhiking, the cities of Plymouth and Chester and of course National Service.

I have to be honest and say that I was not a willing or an enthusiastic conscript when I was called up in 1949. I found myself in a place I didn't want to be in, I was with a group of people I didn't want to be with, and I was doing a job I didn't want to do. I should have had a miserable time. At the time I was convinced I would have been much better off in my comfortable home in Chester. doing an interesting job. In 1951 I could hardly wait to get back home from Plymouth, and yet when I think about it now and I look through my old records, a rather different picture emerges, and this is really the story of this book.

I sent a copy of my original draft to a number of relatives and friends, and I am grateful to all of them for pointing out many errors and for sending me useful additional information. I am indebted to Admiral Sir Derek Reffell for letting me know about the existence of the HMS Wizard and HMS Cadiz Association and the name and address of Shipmate Tom Fox the Hon. Secretary. Both Sir Derek and Tom were kind enough to read my original manuscript and were able to correct me on various points.

I need also to acknowledge the expert technical help I have received from my old firm, Allwoods of Chester and in particular the IT Partner Glyn Hewitt for his work on the photographs and Mrs Karen Hutchins who is a veritable wizard of the word processor. Other aknowledgements are included at the end of the book.

I hope that readers of these memoirs will derive as much pleasure as I have had in putting them together.

CHAPTER ONE

The Carol Concert

Let me start at the end rather than at the beginning. I can pinpoint exactly when I conceived the idea of writing a short account of my time on HMS Wizard in 1950. It was Saturday 14 December 2002 on a coach going to a carol concert at Liverpool. I was sitting next to an old friend who shares my tastes in classical music and the theatre. I mentioned the play "The Dresser" and we started to talk about Donald Wolfit. I said that I had seen him and his company at the Palace Theatre, Plymouth when I had been stationed at Devonport in 1950. I was surprised to learn that my friend had done his National Service in the Royal Navy, as a Sick Berth Attendant from 1947 to 1949. Our conversation ranged over the Carl Rosa Opera Company (which also played at the Palace Theatre), Welsh National Opera, Covent Garden, the Shakespeare Memorial Theatre and much more besides. I mentioned to my friend that I had never had any contact with anyone from my National Service days since I was demobbed in 1951. In fact I could hardly remember anyone's name apart from one little incident in 1982 at the time of the Falklands' Campaign. I was very surprised to open the Daily Telegraph one morning to learn that Rear Admiral Derek Reffell had been appointed to succeed Rear Admiral Sandy Woodward as Naval Task Group Commander. Had his name been John Jones or Peter Robinson it would not have registered, but there had been a Sub-Lieutenant Reffell on board HMS Wizard when I was there in 1950. It must be the same person. I suggested to my wife that I should write him a letter of congratulation on his appointment, but this bright idea was very firmly turned down. I thought it would be a pretty harmless gesture, and might even lead to an invitation to have lunch at the Admiralty!

On the way back to the coach after the concert some other friends, who had been in the seats in front of us, said that they hoped I would not be offended but they could not help overhearing our conversation and particularly the reference to Covent Garden as they were planning a visit there. They mentioned also that they knew Derek Reffell whom they had met when going down to see their daughter. I was amazed that anyone on that coach would know Admiral Sir Derek Reffell.

They have met Admiral Reffell at the end of his distinguished career. He is now Sir Derek, a former Third Sea Lord and Controller of the Navy and a former Governor of Gibraltar. By contrast I knew Derek Reffell in the very early days. I was going to say as a humble, lowly Sub-Lieutenant. I will delete the word humble, because he had recently passed out from Dartmouth, and all those cadets were impressive young men trained to be leaders and were far from humble. Lowly is a word I can use quite properly as you will see when I describe the ship's company in more detail.

This memoir is long on memory and short on detailed research, but I do have a few records which have helped to jog my memory.

When I was demobbed in May 1951, I was informed that, on completion of my whole-time National Service, I had been entered in the Royal Naval Special Reserve until 22 November 1954. I was also told that I had been allowed to retain certain articles of service kit whilst in the RNSR. I was to keep the kit in good condition and take it with me when I reported for training. Furthermore, if I attended with articles of kit missing I would be required to pay for replacements.

I received a further communication from the Office of the Registrar, Royal Naval Special Reserve at Devonport dated 16 November 1954 to the effect that on completion of my whole time and part time service under the National Service Acts 1948-50 I was being retained in the Royal Naval Special Reserve until 30 June 1959, in accordance with the Navy, Army and Air Force Reserve Act 1954. I would no longer have any liability for training and I would only be liable to be called out for service in the event of imminent national danger or of great emergency. I was, however, still required to maintain my uniform in good condition as I would be expected to bring it with me if I were called out.

The serge jackets and trousers issued to us were not very smart for wearing outside of barracks and most of us ordered a tiddly suit from one of the naval tailors (Bernard and Gieves). The more expensive ones were in doeskin but as I was only going to be there for eighteen months I ordered a cheaper alternative in barathea.

In view of the letters from the Admiralty I kept all my release documents safely and these have enabled me to quote precise dates for certain events. If no precise date is given it means that I am relying on memory.

Apart from the release documents I have found old diaries for 1949 and 1951 which have been helpful. I have not found a diary for 1950 but my old Youth Hostels Association Membership card, my extensive collection of old concert and theatre programmes and a few faded newspaper cuttings from that time have helped me fill many gaps. I still have my old passport issued in 1948 and this is useful, as in those days passports were always date-stamped at border crossings.

Although I do not have a diary for 1950, I have found among my old papers the daily sheets I prepared from 2 January 1950 to 8 August 1950. These listed all the jobs I had to do that day: orders to be sent out, deliveries to be accepted, forms to be prepared, signatures and countersignatures to be obtained.

Daily sheet 1st August 1950

4

CHAPTER TWO

Royal Arthur, Ceres and Drake

I celebrated my eighteenth birthday on 21 December 1948 and I was very aware that I was now going to be called up to do my eighteen months National Service.

Many people have asked me how I managed to go into the Royal Navy rather than the army or the airforce. It was quite simple. One of my friends had already been conscripted into the Royal Navy and he strongly advised me to follow his lead. I didn't try to pull any strings. I just ticked the appropriate box on the application form.

On Monday 10 January 1949 I registered for National Service and on Friday 28 January 1949 I had my medical in Liverpool. I got up at 5.30 am as I had to be in Liverpool for 8.30 am. The medical examination was the most comprehensive I had ever had and, having been pronounced AI, I arrived back in Chester at 1.00 pm and went back to the office for the afternoon.

This was a rather unsettling period because I couldn't make any plans for the future. Every day I wondered if the postman might deliver my call-up papers. These eventually arrived on Saturday 7 May 1949 and things then started to move very quickly. I had my last day at work (on an outside audit) on Friday 13 May – no send off or farewell party. I doubt if I even had a handshake from my boss.

I decided to have a short holiday before joining up. My uncle and aunt had a sweetshop in London and my aunt was ill and was in St Mary's Hospital, Paddington. I travelled down to London by train and visited my aunt in hospital some evenings after working in the shop during the day. I also found time to see a film, Cardboard Cavalier starring Margaret Lockwood and Sid Field, a play at the Duchess Theatre, "The Foolish Gentlewoman" and the New London Opera Company production of Tosca at the Stoll Theatre. I think that this performance of Tosca was the most exciting evening I had ever spent in a theatre.

I joined the Royal Navy on 23 May 1949. With my call-up papers was a one-way railway ticket to Corsham in Wiltshire where HMS Royal Arthur was located.

I had a comfortable train journey changing at Bristol and Bath and arrived at Corsham at four o'clock. We were then marched in a body to the camp. It was raining steadily. After tea, a wash and brush up, supper and getting our bedding we had time to look in at the NAAFI and to have a stroll round. My diary records – "slightly unfavourable impression".

HMS Royal Arthur – it has quite a ring to its name doesn't it? Actually it was just like any other nondescript army or airforce camp anywhere in the country, but the Royal Navy has this quaint habit of imagining that these shore bases are afloat. Every one of these stone frigates has an impressive flagstaff and a quarterdeck. The place is organised in watches as if on board a ship – the first watch, the middle watch, the dogwatch etc. You have four bells at 6 o'clock in the morning, eight bells at noon. When you want to go out of the camp you catch a liberty boat to go ashore (yes, miles from the sea in the middle of Wiltshire). It was exactly the same at HMS Ceres (in the middle of Yorkshire) and HMS Drake the huge naval barracks in Devonport.

THE LEEDS GRAND THEATRE PROUDLY PRESENTS THE VERY BEST IN LIVING ENTERTAINMENT

COMMENCING MONDAY, SEPTEMBER 5th, 1949
FOR TWO WEEKS

GRAND OPERA PRODUCTIONS LTD. present

THE CARL ROSA OPERA

Under the direction of H. B. PHILLIPS, C.B.E.

Conductors:
Arthur Hammond, Dr. Frederick Berend, Emanuel Yourovsky,
David Andrews

Carl Ross Orchestra   Leader: Ross Stevsking
Programmes are subject to alteration
Puccini Operas by arrangement with Ricordi & Co.
"Stories of the Operas," obtainable from attendants, price 1/6

SATURDAY EVENING, 10th SEPTEMBER, at 6.30

FAUST

Opera in Five Acts
By JULES BARBIER and MICHEL CARRE
Music by CHARLES GOUNOD

Faust (a learned Doctor) ...... RAYMOND NILSSON
Mephistopheles .... ARTHUR WALLINGTON
Valentine (Brother to Marguerite), ARTHUR COPLEY
Wagner (a Student) .... ERNEST THOMAS
Siebel (a Youth, in love with Marguerite),
                                    BARBARA HOWITT
Martha (Neighbour to Marguerite), MONICA SINCLAIR
Marguerite .... RUTH PACKER
Students, Soldiers, People, Priests, Angels, Demons, etc.
Conductor: ARTHUR HAMMOND

A selection of theatre programmes

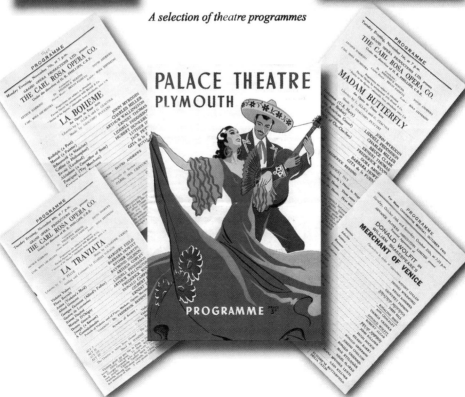

The course of basic training lasted four weeks and I have two photographs as a reminder of those days. The group photograph of Class 1721 does very little to stir my memory. Parcell was a stores assistant from South Wales and would have been with me at Ceres. I think I met him on occasions later on in Devonport. I felt sorry for John Prestwich – he had ambitions to be an opera singer and was worried about damaging his voice. He was most obviously a square peg in a round hole. Evason was from Liverpool and was a steward. I think he might have been posted like me to HMS Wizard. The photograph of Barr, Walton, Dawkins and myself shows me with three recruits I clearly related to. Possibly we were all ex-grammar school boys. Johnny Barr was the outstanding member of the class, definitely officer material. I sometimes wondered what the other characters in the group photograph went on to achieve in later life.

Chief Petty Officer Batchelor was in charge of our class. He was not very tall and a typical weather-beaten old salt. He knew every trick in the trade and his knowing looks left you in no doubt. He had become, with his long years of experience, quite a clever amateur psychologist and was a cunning operator always many steps ahead of a band of raw recruits. He very quickly identified Searle as the potential "comedian" in the class and once he had got him into line the rest was plain sailing. He employed a clever mixture of the carrot and stick approach, with really biting, hurtful sarcasm and ridicule on occasions. He was doing an excellent job. He very quickly licked us into shape. We were soon transformed on the parade ground from an unruly, undisciplined rabble into a smart, respectable unit. We were all a little frightened of him, but at the same time we quite liked him. Quite an achievement I think.

The Supply and Secretariat ratings were posted to Wetherby, Yorkshire to join HMS Ceres on 28 June 1949 to undergo their specialist training. We travelled by train, changing at Bristol and Leeds. It was a boiling hot day. I have no photographs for that period. 1949 was a very hot summer and we did our square-bashing in intense heat. We also had to take a turn at guard duties, and I can remember my distaste at being on guard round the perimeter fence in the small hours of the morning. We were on watch for four hours, and even on a summer night I didn't enjoy being on my own in the middle of nowhere, somewhere in Yorkshire.

I have pleasant memories of visiting various places near to Wetherby. Harrogate, Knaresborough, Tadcaster, Ripon, Leeds and York. I don't think that Wetherby itself held much in the way of attraction. I thought that York with its Minster had a better Cathedral than Chester, but Chester my native city had infinitely more impressive walls.

I was particularly keen to get into Leeds to the Grand Theatre when the Carl Rosa Opera Company played there. I saw La Traviata on the Tuesday, La Boheme on the Thursday and Faust on the Saturday. I thought that Faust was a pretty poor opera but I had enjoyed the other two. I still have the programmes. For opera buffs I can mention that the leading singers in those days were Raymond Nilsson, Arthur Copley, Margery Field, Gita de la Fuente and Ruth Packer.

When we enlisted in May 1949 we were allocated to one of the Home Commands – Chatham, Devonport or Portsmouth. Everybody knows that Portsmouth is Pompey, but not so many know that Devonport is Guzz. Once I had been posted to my home base of Devonport I never met any ratings from Portsmouth or Chatham. It was as if the Devonport ratings made up their own separate bit of the navy.

Our courses at Ceres finished on Friday 16 September and we then had to go through the standard draft routine ready for travelling south to Plymouth on Tuesday 20 September. The journey began at 0730 and we got to King's Cross Station in London at about 1400. We had a little time to kill in London before making our way across the capital to Paddington Station for the direct train to Plymouth. We arrived at Plymouth sometime after 2200 and had to go through part of our joining routine in HMS Drake in the pouring rain, finally getting into our hammocks shortly after midnight (2400). The joining routine would continue over the next day or so and then we were allocated to our jobs.

I disliked these enormous impersonal barracks and tried to go ashore into Plymouth at every available opportunity. There was really no work for us to do – it was a transit camp, but we had to look as if we were busy! I spent a lot of time reading and writing letters home to my family and friends. I was particularly pleased when Donald Wolfit and his company came to the Palace Theatre at the end of October and I saw him in Macbeth, King Lear and the Merchant of Venice. The following week the Carl Rosa Opera Company arrived and I saw Carmen, Madame Butterfly, Rigoletto, La Boheme and the Barber of Seville. All this theatre going blew a hole in my finances and I had to write to my mother for some cash, and she sent me £3.

After six or seven weeks of this tedious hanging about in barracks I was very excited to learn on Monday 7 November that I was being posted to HMS Wizard. The customary draft routine started straight away. Early on the morning of Monday 14 November I reported to the draft office (DFDO). I packed my kit bag and hammock and after lunch went on a Motor Fishing Vessel with all the other ratings with new postings. I was the last to be dropped off as they couldn't find the Wizard hiding behind Drake's Island in the Sound.

Arthur Dawkins, Ray Williams, John Barr and John Walton
at HMS Royal Arthur May 1949

8

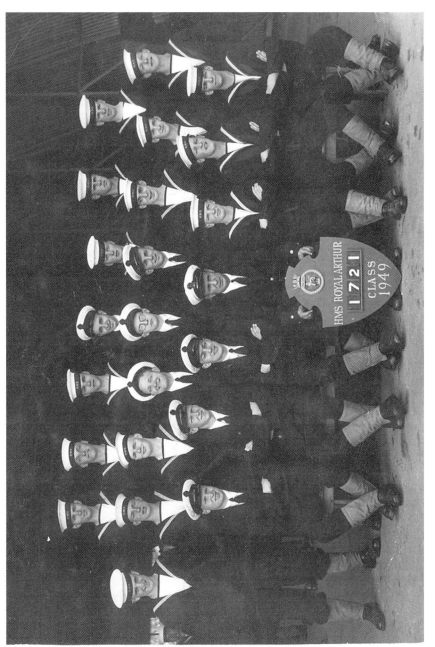

1721 Class HMS Royal Arthur May 1949

9

CHAPTER THREE

The Ship's Company

When I joined HMS Wizard there were seven officers in the Ward Room:-
The Captain (the Old Man)
The First Lieutenant (Jimmy the One)
The Navigating Officer
The Engineering Officer
The Electrical Officer
The Gunner (TAS) – short for Torpedo anti-submarine
Sub-Lieutenant Reffell.
My first Captain was Commander J H Eaden DSC and Bar. I remember the atmosphere on board the ship when he left. He was obviously an outstanding officer, a born leader of men. All the CPO's and PO's were unanimous in singing his praises and regretted his departure. I don't think that this always happens on a change of Captain. Commander Eaden left in mid-March 1950 and our new Captain was Commander J D Hayes DSO. He, like his predecessor, had done well in the Second World War. The buzz on the messdeck was that he had had a fairly cushy number in Whitehall and that he was not wildly excited about being given the command of a sea-going ship. The officers thought that he was pleased to be at sea, but would have preferred a more exciting command than Wizard in the Plymouth Local Squadron.
The First Lieutenant was Lt Cdr R R Colls and he was universally respected by the ship's company, officers and men alike. He was not an unfriendly man, but he was by nature a man of few words. A bluff, no-nonsense sort of man. His stock, which was already high, rose even higher at the time of our visit to Ilfracombe.
The Navigating Officer was Lieutenant Graeme M Lloyd. Tall, fresh faced, possibly fair-haired. I would not have remembered his name if he had not signed my History Sheet. I cannot resist the temptation of quoting his comments when I left the Wizard in November 1950.
"An excellent Stores Assistant who performed his duties in a most capable and efficient manner".
Obviously a very perceptive officer who would go far!
The Gunner (TAS) was Taffy Lawrence a Commissioned Officer (one thin gold ring) and addressed as Mister. He wore highly polished black gaiters and the other officers called him Guns.
Sub-Lieutenant Reffell was recently out of Dartmouth and this was one of his first postings to a sea-going ship. I felt sorry for him at times, as he was a bit of a dogsbody for the Captain and the other more senior officers. He had to be very alert as the Chief Petty Officers and Petty Officers had all been in the Royal Navy during the war and had plenty of medals and badges to show for it. These hoary old seadogs would be waiting for any slips made by a young Sub-Lieutenant freshly out of Dartmouth. On the other hand, Sub-Lieutenant Reffell would have benefited greatly by serving under such a fine experienced officer as Lt Cdr Colls.

The Chief Petty Officers had their own mess. My "boss" was the CPO Coxswain but he took very little interest in what I was doing so long as everything was running smoothly. It would have been a different story if anything had gone wrong. I think the Coxswain had a wide variety of responsibilities. We were not big enough to have our own medical officer on board, and I don't think that we had a Sick Berth Attendant either. The Coxswain was responsible therefore for medical matters. He was important also in the maintenance of discipline. Any miscreants would be brought before the Captain or the First Lieutenant by the Coxswain.

The only other Chief Petty Officer I can still see very clearly in my mind was Bungy Williams the Chief Stoker. I didn't realise what an important person he was until one day the ship was diverted off its course into Fowey so that the Chief could go ashore for his week-end leave. I doubt if such a concession would have been made for anyone else. He was also renowned as a champion wrestler.

The Petty Officers also had their own mess. I was in Mess 7, the odds and sods. There were three Cooks, a Writer and two other Stores Assistants. The Signals and Wireless/ Telegraphy bods were in Mess No 1.

The biggest messes were of course for the seamen and stokers.

At the back of my mind I have a figure of 200 as the total ship's company, but I find it difficult to believe that that is right. We also had a NAAFI manager (always referred to as the Canteen Damager) on board. He was a civilian and was in the Petty Officers' Mess.

I remember that there was a good spirit and camaraderie in the mess. The occasional practical joke and leg-pull, the arguments (probably between Liverpool and Everton supporters), the earnest discussions on occasions.

I would not want to convey the impression that all was sweetness and light, and that life was a bed of roses. You had to watch your belongings like a hawk as thieving was widespread. If something was not nailed down to the messdeck table it was regarded by some as public property. Also I never got used to the foul language prevalent on board. It still jars whenever I see a film or a play with a lot of bad language.

There were also a lot of minor rackets and fiddles going on, arising partly from the fact that there was still food and clothing rationing in force in the country. Some items of naval clothing (the raincoats, shirts, collars and socks) were equally suitable for civilian wear, and a lot of these items got into civilian hands. Also anyone with access to food supplies might be tempted to supplement the meagre rations of their relatives and friends. I'm thinking particularly of the stewards, chefs and Jack Dusties. It was no temptation to me as I didn't have any relatives or friends in Plymouth.

There was always a certain amount of smuggling duty free goods ashore, particularly cigarettes and tickler (tins of tobacco for roll your own cigarettes using RIZLA cigarette papers). Contraband was affectionately known as rabbits.

One of the Jack Dusties had recently been released from Naval prison after serving three months' imprisonment for smuggling cigarettes. His graphic account of life inside a navy gaol certainly made a great impression on me, and may have had an effect on others in the mess. The punishment had certainly been excessive in relation to the monetary value of excise duty saved, but the punitive nature of the sentence certainly was an effective deterrent.

I suspected that some of my shipmates had come from Barnardos. Quite a few had been to HMS Ganges (near Ipswich) as boy seamen, and had signed on regular engagements when they were eighteen. The odd one or two may have had experience of other educatíonal establishments, maybe Borstal or Approved Schools. Some of my messmates were from the toughest parts of Scotland Road in Liverpool and the Gorbals in Glasgow. You wouldn't pick a fight with them; they were a harder and tougher type than I had ever previously met. I am sure that the Royal Navy, with its strict uncompromising discipline, was the making of them.

I never had the opportunity to go to university, because of the abnormal situation in the late forties when all the returning ex-servicemen obviously had to have priority. Possibly my two years away from home serving on the Lower Deck was quite a good substitute for a spell at university.

I don't remember having a particular friend (or oppo) on board except possibly Scribes (Writer Jack Jones). I would go ashore with whoever happened to be off-duty and this could be either a Regular or a National Serviceman. There was no distinction between us; we were all treated alike.

EMPLOYMENT RECORD.

NOTE:—To be filled up on termination of service under a particular Accountant Officer. The record is not normally to be completed in respect of periods of less than three months. The Accountant Officer may, however, at his discretion make an entry for a shorter period if he has particular reasons for so doing.

SHIP	Rating	Date		Capacity in which employed*	Remarks as to ability, special qualifications Any special knowledge and characteristics Record of examinations passed	Signature of Accountant Officer if of Paymaster-Lieutenant's rank or above ; otherwise Captain
		From	To			
1	2	3	4	5	6	(11) 7
CERES	P.S.A.	28.6.49	19.9.49	U.T.	Date of passing Pt.11 N.E.Crse. 16th Sept. '49. Marks Obtained: Vict.124/175; Clo. & M.T. 94/100; Naval Stores 155/175;Total 403/450 = 89%.Suitable for draft to small ships.	*illegible signature* CAPTAIN (S)
WIZARD	P.S.A. S.A.	15/8/49 21/9/	20/10/49	Victualling	An excellent S.A. who performed his duties in a most capable and efficient manner.	G. M. Lloyd L/EST. RN.
ORION (Home)	S.A. = L.S.A.(V)	20/1/50		Victualling	Agree entirely with above. A keen & energetic worker who gives of his best without supervision.	Brotherwee Paib-Ed (S)
INDEFATIGABLE	LSA(V)	8.6.52	27.6.52	Victualling.	A quiet and efficient rating. Has done very well during his period of training.	Je Robertson L.t.(S)

*Specific notations should be made—Central Storekeeping (Store Rooms or Accounts), Clothing, Victualling (Store Rooms or Accounts) specifying General Messing or Standard Ration, etc.

Jack Dusty

The Royal Navy (the Andrew) has a penchant for calling things by colourful nicknames. The Army and the Airforce have a similar patois. Stores Assistants were always called Jack Dusties. I always felt it was rather an affectionate nickname for us. Writers are Scribes, Cooks are Chefs (what else?), Electricians are Sparks and Signallers are Buntings.

I was the only Stores Assistant (Victualling) on board HMS Wizard and I had to order all the supplies of food that were needed. This involved getting the signals' ratings (possibly the CPO, or Yeoman as he was called) to relay my orders. There were regular deliveries from the Admiralty Cold Store and Royal William Yard at Plymouth. Bread always came from S Stephens and milk was delivered daily by Plymouth Co-operative Society, Radnor Dairy when we were in Guzz. There was a list of authorised suppliers at different ports when we needed bread or vegetables. I had an ordinary seaman assigned to me to do some of the donkey work. His nickname was the Tanky, but in official parlance he was called a butcher. When we had a big delivery I would need a small gang of seamen to move the boxes from the dockside up the gangway into my stores. Our ship had a system of catering called "canteen messing" – each mess prepared its own food which was then taken to the galley for the chefs to cook. There was a rota on each mess as to who would be "Cook of the Shack" that day. A similar rota existed for the daily cleaning of the messdeck and tables. Each mess had a standard allowance based on their numbers of what could be spent on food, and it was one of my jobs to account for this. Each month I prepared my accounts for submission to base at Devonport. I would sign these and have them countersigned by the Coxswain, the First Lieutenant and the Captain. The Writer (Scribes) would have the job of sending the monthly returns to base. I wonder if any of my accounts are preserved in the Naval archives at Devonport.

The First Lieutenant was the Victualling Officer and I tended to deal directly with him most of the time. I am certain that the Coxswain did not mind being bypassed in this way. When it came to any cash received (sales of soap and tobacco, clothing and cap tallies) this had to be given to Sub-Lieutenant Reffell, the Cash Officer.

I had my own little office (caboosh) immediately forward of the NAAFI on the port side of the vessel.

One little incident I do recall after all these years was when I was summoned to appear before Sub-Lieutenant Reffell for a breach of King's Rules and Regulations (later altered to King's Rules and Admiralty Instructions). On his routine rounds of the ship as duty officer, Sub-Lieutenant Reffell had spotted that the door of the spud locker was open and an explanation was needed. I was reprimanded for this breach of discipline, but no record was made on my conduct sheet and no loss of privileges was suffered. There were just a few measly old potatoes in the locker, hardly worth pinching. I'm quite sure it was Tanky's fault, but I was the one who "carried the can".

One of my main duties was to organise the daily issue of the tots of rum. I was tempted to say "preside over" but that would not be correct. This time-honoured ritual was far too important to allow me to do that. On every ship in the Royal Navy at 12 noon the bubbly would be issued by the Jack Dusty to a representative of each mess. The Officer of the Day would be there, together with the Coxswain and possibly the Duty Petty Officer. Distribution took place from my office.

For the Chief Petty Officers and Petty Officers the rum was issued in its neat form. All other ratings got their daily ration as grog, a diluted form of 1 part rum to 2 parts water. Teetotallers received threepence per day in lieu of their rum ration.

The rum issue was stopped in 1970 many years after I had left the Royal Navy. It certainly had a soporific effect on some of the ratings – much less work was done after lunch.

The little ceremony each day at 12 noon was a small but useful chance for an amicable exchange of news and views between the Wardroom and the Lower Deck. In those few relaxed minutes the latest ship's gossip would spread very effectively.

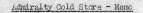

Admiralty Cold Store - Memo

    As a temporary arrangement the Vegetable Contractor will supply on Fridays, commencing March 17th, 1950, broccoli for weekend issue in lieu of cabbage.

    For accounting purposes the broccoli will be invoiced as cabbage.

    All Supply Officers requiring supplies should forward demands for cabbage (broccoli) to reach the Cold Store no later than 1600 Wednesday for supply the following Friday.

                           Surveyor of Food Supplies
                for Superintending Victualling Store Officer

                    13/3/50.

The Supply Officer,

    H.M.S. WIZARD,

        DEVONPORT.

PMP.

SLOPS

Revised prices of clothing - March 1950

Issuing Prices of Clothing

Action working dress:

Item	Unit	Price
Shirts	ea	10/9
Trousers	pr	12/5
Belts, waist, blue	ea	1/8
Belts, waist, white	ea	1/9
Caps, blue, oval, Class II	ea	4/9
Caps, blue, round, Class II	ea	3/8
Cases, attaché	ea	7/9
Cases, suit	ea	34/2
Collars, seamens blue	ea	2/9
Drawers, cotton, E.T.	pr	2/9
Handkerchiefs, white, cotton	ea	8^d
Jerseys, seaman	ea	12/9
Overall combination suits, blue	ea	11/9
Shoes, black, leather	pr	24/9
Shoes, gymnasium	pr	6/3
Socks, thin, blue	pr	2/1
Socks, thick, blue	pr	1/11
Socks, white, cotton	pr	11^d
Towels, seamen's	ea	2/10
Vests, summer	ea	2/2
Scarves, black, silk	ea	1/10

Issuing prices of less common items obtainable from Victualling Office before "Out pipes" Wednesday forenoon.

S80's to be handed in (by leading hands) to Coxwain's Office by 0900 Wednesday.

CHAPTER FIVE

Springtime in Paris

By May 1950 I was entitled to annual leave and I decided to go to Paris rather than home to Chester. I had to obtain special permission to go abroad during my National Service and this was granted on the strict understanding that I did not wear my naval uniform whilst in France. I am trying to work out why I did this. I had been to Paris for two weeks in the summer of 1948 and it must have made a powerful impression on me. I had stayed with the Calmus family, as their son Daniel was my sister's penfriend and he had been to Chester in 1947.

The French seemed to be recovering from the war more quickly than we were. Life in Paris in 1948 was quickly getting back to normal. I was horrified to see that in their butchers and grocers the housewives had an open choice between buying with their ration cards or purchasing on the black market. In England black market trading was very definitely under the counter.

Dan Calmus took me to all the usual tourist places – the Champs Elysee, l'arc de Triomphe, Montmartre, Pigalle, Sacré Coeur, Place Vendome, Les Invalides, the Madeleine, Tour Eiffel, Bois de Boulogne, Notre Dame, Place de la Concorde, Versailles and the Louvre. We went to see a tennis match at Stade Roland Garros. I think I probably went on my own to see Fidelio at the opera. I was quite shocked when we went to the cinema that we had to give a tip to the usherette for showing us to our seats. I can't remember if Dan took me to see the Folies Bergeres. I had a really memorable holiday and I think that I must have decided to go back to the wonderful city of Paris as soon as I could.

I had been an enthusiastic member of the Youth Hostels Association since 1946 and had done a lot of hitchhiking in North Wales and the Peak District. So I decided to go hitchhiking to France and to revisit Paris.

Looking back after all these years I must confess that I am surprised that I went on my own. I am not by nature a person who likes going to places on his own. Whenever I go to a play, a concert or a film it will always be with someone else. I would never go to a football match or a cricket match on my own. I would always team up with someone else.

I have been able to reconstruct the basic dates and details of my trip to France from my YHA membership card, my theatre programmes and the old passport.

I rented a locker for two weeks at the Agnes Weston Seamens' Home as we were not allowed to leave the Wizard in civilian clothes. My leave started on Monday 15 May and I stayed at Exeter Youth Hostel that night. The next day I hitchhiked to Tillingbourne Youth Hostel and on Wednesday I was in Brighton and went to the Theatre Royal to see the play "If this be error" by Rachel Grieve. Mary Ellis, Clive Morton and Gladys Henson were in the cast, as was a very young Nicholas Parsons. I caught the Newhaven – Dieppe Ferry on Thursday 18 May and stayed in Paris for a week. I have three theatre programmes for L'Opéra Comique. None of the names of the main artistes rings a bell. I stayed two nights at the Youth Hostel at Rouen and three nights at the Youth Hostel at St Valery-en-Caux. I sailed back to England from Dieppe on Tuesday 30 May and stayed at the Central London Youth Hostel. I spent the following day in London before catching the train from Paddington to Plymouth. I have a very interesting theatre programme for a matinee performance of The Winter's Tale at the Open Air Theatre in Regents Park.

16

Robert Atkins (the actor manager and producer) played Autolycus and Henry McGee and Leslie Crowther had minor parts.

On reaching Plymouth Station I made my way to Aggie Westons to get back into uniform before reporting back to ship.

There was a curious episode during my stay in Paris, and I have two small black and white photographs as evidence of it. I made friends with a young Scottish couple and went sight-seeing with them. Their names have long since been forgotten, so I have to think of suitable nicknames. My first thought was Bonnie and Clyde as it sounded Scottish, but this must be rejected because of B and C's criminal activities. The best alternative I can come up with is Jock and Jill. How on earth did I get to know Jock and Jill? Perhaps they were staying at the Youth Hostel in Paris. I am convinced that they were married because in 1950 respectable young ladies like Jill just did not go away on holiday with their boyfriends. If they were married, could they have been on their honeymoon in Paris? A little bit farfetched taking into account the strictly segregated dormitories in all youth hostels. Perhaps I just met them at a boulevard café. I can't remember if they felt sorry for a young Englishman on his own in Paris and took me under their wing, or if I volunteered to show them round the sights. After all, I had been in Paris for two weeks in 1948 and knew my way round. We must have exchanged addresses because after I got back to the Wizard I received two photographs inscribed in Jill's writing May 1950 – taken at Versailles and May 1950 Colonial Museum, Paris. The old passport, apart from recording border crossings, also includes details of Foreign Exchange obtained from the bank for each holiday. For my 1948 holiday I obtained £8 worth of French francs at Westminster Bank at Newhaven. For the 1950 holiday I got £15 worth of French francs from the Westminster Bank at Brighton. I was a big spender even in those days.

The Summer Term 1950 edition of The Inkwell gives details of a visit to Paris by my old School at Easter 1950 – we had missed each other by about six weeks.

THÉATRE NATIONAL DE L'OPÉRA COMIQUE

Notre Dame

CHAPTER SIX

Summer Programme 1950

I don't know if the Royal Navy still do this – they possibly haven't got enough ships these days – but we went to different ports so that we could show the flag. Our programme for that summer was as follows:

Monday 7 August to
Sunday 13 August   St Peter's Port, Guernsey

Monday 14 August to
Sunday 20 August   Ilfracombe

Monday 21 August to
Saturday 26 August   Cardiff

Sunday 27 August to
Friday 1 September   Paignton

Tuesday 5 September to
Saturday 9 September   Torquay (for Babbacombe Regatta)

Thursday 21 September to
Monday 25 September   Dartmouth

I remember little about Cardiff, Paignton, Torquay or Dartmouth but I do have happy memories of going to Guernsey. Why should I retain strong memories of that particular week and not any of the others? I have included at the end of this chapter the detailed programme for the visit to St Peter's Port. Apart from those events I still have the programme for the Little Theatre, Central Hall production of "Worm's Eye View" by R F Delderfield with the Denville Players. The cast was led by Roy Dotrice.
I remember the coach trip round the island, the extra strong beer and the cricket match we played there. I wonder if St Peter's Port Cricket Club still have their score book for 1950 – and who played and who won?
The standard of cricket must have been pretty ropey – none of us would have had our own bats, boots or batting gloves. I always associate Sub-Lieutenant Reffell with the cricket matches we played. He was the Sports Officer and was probably the Captain and our best player. Also, where on earth did we get the bats and pads and other gear from? The ship's Welfare Fund apparently paid for the equipment.

Paignton Urban District Council produced a special card for the visit of HMS Wizard. A full programme of matches against local civilian teams was arranged in cricket, billiards, water polo, darts, snooker and hockey. I made a note on my card that the cricket match arranged for 2.30pm on Monday 28 August 1950 versus Paignton CC in Queen's Park was postponed owing to rain. Possibly we managed to play later in the week.

The visit to Ilfracombe was notable for our hasty departure from that resort. Everybody who was not required for watchkeeping duties had gone ashore. The ship was at anchor in the bay as there was no quayside to tie up alongside. I had gone to the cinema, and near the end of the film a message was flashed on to the screen to say that all ratings from HMS Wizard were to return to the ship immediately. The weather was deteriorating, the wind was getting up and the ship's anchor was dragging on the rocky sea bottom. The whole of the north coast of Devon is very rocky and something urgent had to be done. Orders would have been sought from Devonport and it had been decided that we should steam through the night to the safe refuge of Milford Haven.

I cannot remember if everyone ashore managed to make it back to the ship, but I can remember the First Lieutenant, Lt Cdr Colls barking out his orders as we prepared to set off into the night, head on into a really fierce gale. It was a scary few hours and I remember the sense of relief that everyone felt when in the early hours of the following morning we looked out of our portholes and realised that we had reached the calm and safe confines of Milford Haven. It is probably an exaggeration to say this, but I have always thought that we all owed our lives to Lt Cdr Colls that night.

The other ships in our flotilla, HMS Ulster, HMS Roebuck and HMS Burghead Bay also had visits to various places. The Burghead Bay in fact joined the Wizard at St Peter's Port for the visit to Guernsey.

GUERNSEY

The Programme at St Peter's Port

Monday 7 August

0730   Sail Devonport.

1500   Arrive St Peter Port.

1530   Government Secretary (Major-General R F Colwill, CBE) accompanied by Captain Brock, RN Retd, Vice-President, States Reception Committee, the Chief Officer of Police, Mr Lamy, the Revs Moore and Bedford representing the local Church of England and Free Churches Association, the Harbour Master, Captain Nicolle, and the Secretary to States' Committees, calls to discuss programme.

Tuesday 8 August

1030   Commanding Officers call on His Excellency the Lieutenant Governor (Lieutenant General Sir Philip Neame, VC, KBE, CB, DSO) followed by call on Deputy Bailiff of Guernsey (Jurat Quertier le Pelley).

1200   His Excellency the Lieutenant Governor returns call.

1230   Deputy Bailiff returns call.

1430   100 ratings (50 Wizard and 50 Burghead Bay) go on bus tour of island – Buses leave from White Rock at the Harbour.

1830   Cocktail Party in Wizard – 70 guests.

        Evening Variety Entertainment (25 tickets).

Wednesday 9 August

1430   100 ratings go on bus tour.

        Evening Variety Entertainment (25 tickets).

Saturday 12 August

1500   Whaler Race – Wizard, Burghead Bay and RN Association crews.

2000 – 2200
        Ships' Companies entertained at Masonic Hall – Numbers not known.

NOTES

(1)   Both Ships will be open to visitors from 1400 – 1730, Tuesday to Saturday inclusive. (Local Boats will be used).

(2)   A Cricket Match and a Swimming Meeting with a Water Polo Match have been arranged. Details of time and place are not known.

(3)   Variety Entertainment (Professional) Twenty-five free tickets are being given to the two ships for the concerts at Candie Gardens on Tuesday and Wednesday.

(4)   There are 4 swimming pools close to the Harbour known as La Valette. These are free of charge except for the mixed pool, where a 6d entrance fee is charged.

(5)   Libertymen are warned the beer on the Island is much stronger than on the mainland.

(6)   The Old Government House Hotel and Royal Hotel are reserved for Officers.

CHAPTER SEVEN

Other Visits

We were involved in the State Visit to this country in March 1950 of the French President Vincent Auriol. He came over in a French warship from Calais to Dover and was escorted by other French warships to the halfway point in the English Channel. HMS Wizard and other warships met the French ships in mid-channel and escorted the French President into Dover harbour. We had to line the rails on the upper deck and give him three rousing cheers while waving our caps. We had practised this routine many times beforehand. I imagine we also escorted the French warship back to the middle of the English Channel after his visit and gave him another three cheers! While we were in Dover I remember it gave me the opportunity to visit Canterbury Cathedral for the first time.

We went to Birkenhead in June 1950 to escort the aircraft carrier HMS Illustrious for the launch of HMS Ark Royal by the then Queen (our present Queen's mother). As soon as we docked in Birkenhead I got ashore as quickly as possible and headed for Woodside or Rock Ferry to catch a train or a Crosville bus to Chester.

I suppose that it's not very patriotic or loyal to say so but I was not terribly interested in the launching of the Ark Royal. I was much keener to escape from naval routine back to my congenial civilian home life for a few hours. Throughout I was subconsciously a civilian rather than a serviceman. I have no recollection of being present at the launch of the Ark Royal, but I have found an article in the Summer Term 1950 edition of The Inkwell, the magazine of my old School. This is reproduced as a separate chapter later on.

When I returned to rejoin the Wizard she had moved to a new berth and I had this nightmare scenario, wandering round the vast poorly lit and deserted Birkenhead docks trying to find my ship before my leave expired.

I remember with great clarity the visit we paid to the French port of Cherbourg. We were scheduled to stay in Cherbourg for three or four days but many of us only went ashore on the first evening. When we started drinking in the French bars, we realised that their range of drinks was somewhat broader than our usual pubs in Plymouth or Devonport. This was the first time that I had seen a bright green drink on offer – crème de menthe. Also I learnt that anisette was an attractive drink and not a popular child's sweet. I also came across Cointreau and Curacao for the first time in Cherbourg. Prompted by the barmaid we all had a marvellous evening trying out these strange drinks, with entirely foreseeable consequences. I know I had the mother and father of a hangover the next morning – I felt quite ill and made no further trips ashore. The visit to Cherbourg must have been rather more important than the ones to English ports as we flew the flag of C in C Plymouth, Admiral MacGregor (Wee Mac).

We spent Sunday 16 July in Cawsand Bay having intensive whaler crew practices as we had to be in Dartmouth on 26 July 1950 for the Plymouth Flotilla Regatta. I include a copy of the scores attained on that memorable day. I was not in the Miscellaneous Crew. The little experience I had had in the whaler put me off small boats and sailing for life. I may have been a scorer as all the results have been entered so carefully. My elder sister was moving house recently and clearing away old papers in her desk and unearthed a letter

I had sent to her in July 1950 apologising for not being able to attend her 21st birthday party.

We also tried to pay a visit to Londonderry and got within sight of land when a real pea-souper of a fog descended and it was decided to sail away. I had never been to Ireland and felt cheated out of a visit there.

	1 E.R. Ch. & P.O's 0900 c/a 0830			2 MISCELL. 0925 c/a 0855			3 SEAMEN Ch. & P.O's 0950 c/a 0920			4 VETERANS 1015 c/a 0945			5 SEAMEN 1040 c/a 1010			6 WARDROOM 1105 c/a 1035			
	DRAW	PLACE	POINTS	DRAW	PLACE	POINTS	DRAW	PLACE	POINTS	DRAW	PLACE	POINTS	DRAW	PLACE	POINTS	DRAW	PLACE	POINTS	
WIZARD	4	2	6	2	1	8	2	3	4	3	4	2	4	2	6	2	1	8	34
ROEBUCK	3	4	2	3	3	4	1	2	6	4	3	4	2	3	4	4	4	2	22
ULSTER	2	3	4	1	4	2	3	1	8	1	2	6	1	4	2	3	3	4	28
BURGHEAD BAY	1	1	8	4	2	6	4	4	2	2	1	8	3	1	8	1	2	6	38

NOTES FOR CREWS

1. Tows will start from the stern of the Flotilla.
2. Boats must be waiting for tows before the end of the previous race.
3. Alternate whalers are to be used in the forenoon.
4. The Draw is numbered from the Left, looking towards the Finish, i.e. No. 1 is the eastern boat.

START.

1. Flagstaff on Jetty to No. 8 buoy
2. Under Starter's Orders when Preparative Flag is hauled up. Pay attention to loud-hailer.
3. Start on gun.

FINISH.

Line is from "Wizard" to Flagstaff on shore. It is diagonal, so keep pulling till you are signalled as over by gun or loud-hailer.

		7 BOYS 1400 c/a 1330		8 STOKERS 1440 c/a 1410		9 Young Sea. 1520 c/a 1450	
WIZARD	1	6		4		8	
	2	1		7		6	
ROEBUCK	1	5		2		4	
	2	2		3		3	
ULSTER	1	3		6		1	
	2	7		5		2	
B'H'D. BAY	1	8		1		7	
	2	4		8		5	

Backers' and Spectators' Points

Forenoon—Winner 8 points.
Second 6 ,,
Third 4 ,,
Last 2 ,,

Afternoon—Winner 16 points and so on

All-Comers do NOT count for the Cock.

Tote.—The Tote dividend includes the stake.

Maximum stake on any race £1.

WIZ.	ROE.	ULST.	B. BAY

THE COCK .... WIZARD

ALL-COMERS' CUP .... ULSTER

COLOURS.

Wizard ... ... White
Roebuck ... ... Yellow
Ulster ... ... Blue
Burghead Bay ... ... Green

23

S A Williams R.R.
DMX 877094
7 mess
H.M.S. Wizard
c/o F.M.O. Devonport
Plymouth

Wednesday 19th July 1950

Dear Dil,

Just a line to wish you many, many happy returns - in case I can't get ashore to buy a card. I do hope your party went off bang - and I'm wild about the way I had to spend the week-end - instead of celebrations in the Metropolis. As planned we set sail for FOWEY on Friday afternoon and anchored just off shore (about a mile). Shore leave was granted at five minutes notice - half-a- dozen ratings only having the requisite ability to get cleaned in the time. A storm was brewing on Friday night and whipped up to full force on Saturday. This prevented any of the following from taking place:-
   1) Whaler pulling practice for Flotilla regatta.
   2) Paint-ship.
   3) A run ashore.

We were marooned out there unable to do a thing except "mope". Sunday morning at 0630 we moved back to Plymouth - but not alongside where you could get ashore - oh! no. But to a remote creek - Cawsand Bay - where the whalers' crews spent all Sunday at intensive practice. Now this is moderately boring to the crews themselves. How much more so would you expect it to be to those not in a crew? And how much more even than that to one who may otherwise have had a spiffing week-end? What a rigid impersonal - and I'm afraid at time, inhuman-life this is! Never mention FOWEY to me.

This week we're doing routine Emergency Destroyer Duty in Plymouth Sound. Next week all the Flotilla assembles in the River DART and the REGATTA takes place. I think most interest will centre round the Burghead Bay's TOTALISATOR (maximum stake £1) than the races intrinsically. I have absolutely nothing whatever to do with this affair. I regard it as a chance to get ashore at Dartmouth and Kingswear, and explore a little in that area. Also a chance to advance my bookwork - as the end of the month draws nigh! We then have another week in Plymouth – and after being on show over August week-end (NAVY DAYS) commence our summer cruise proper by a week in Guernsey (St. Petersport) .... but more of that anon.

Mum informs me that you are going home tomorrow - and Margaret & Gillian I believe. You lucky people .... Six weeks of paid leave in a somniferous city like Chester ...... Tell mum and A Edie I'm OK - having received their letters & stamps, not requiring anything and will write later.
   Your loving brother,

   Raymond

ps   Mum has your present - Safe custody I did actually buy it months ago!

CHAPTER EIGHT

The Milford Viscount

HMS Wizard got its name in the newspapers in April 1950. I still have a few faded press cuttings from that time. A Welsh trawler, the Milford Viscount, under Captain Alex Smith and with a crew of 13 had left Milford Haven on March 29 and had called briefly at Castletown Berehaven, County Cork on March 30. She had then set out for the Porculine fishing grounds about 130 miles off the Irish coast and had been due back at Milford Haven on 16 April.

What captured the imagination of the press was that after she was thought to be missing there were reports of faint radio signals being picked up by other trawlers and amateur radio enthusiasts around the country, and this raised hopes that the crew might be safe. HMS Wizard was dispatched to the west coast of Ireland and spent a number of days combing a vast area of the sea. Other ships and trawlers took part together with three RAF Lancasters from Leuchars in Fife.

The Admiralty denied that it had been uncooperative in the earlier days of the search. As far as I can recall, no trace of the trawler or its crew was ever found.

These few days in rough weather in the Atlantic were in fact the main sea-going experience of my two years service in the Royal Navy.

Radios silenced for trawler

NAVAL headquarters at Devonport last night asked all wireless operators, ashore and afloat, for one hour's radio silence from midnight until one o'clock this morning.

The request applied to all warships, merchant ships and amateur radio operators.

It was made to giver the powerful listening station at Land's End a chance to pick up any signal from the trawler Milford Viscount, now missing for 14 days.

This step was taken because previously reported signals from the trawler have been so weak that her position could not be picked up.

A naval officer said last night that the trawler's batteries must be nearly exhausted. "Even the turning of a wireless knob could completely ruin receipt of a signal."

The decision was taken after what was described as a day of ominous silence.

Searching aircraft had flown over thousands of square miles of the Atlantic. The destroyer Wizard had ploughed her way down the Irish coast for hundreds of miles. All reported "no luck yet."

Admiralty Denial

Earlier, the Admiralty, denying that it had been unco-operative in the earlier days of the search, said that the effort provided by aircraft and other trawlers was such that the assistance of a frigate or a destroyer would have been of little value.

When signals were reported from the missing trawler, ships were sent immediately.

CHAPTER NINE

The Launch of the Ark Royal

The shipyard was gradually filling up. It was divided into sections, according to the colour of the tickets, and at the bow of the "ARK" was a platform ten feet high, decorated in red and white, on which was the dais from which Her Majesty Queen Elizabeth would launch the ship. The crowd was subdued and expectant, though a bit excited. There would be, every now and again, a burst of cheering and flags and streamers would be waved violently as the cameramen took the newsreel pictures. Meanwhile, this scene was surveyed by dockers from two flanking ships used as grandstands, to which they clung like flies. These ships were tiny in comparison with the "ARK ROYAL", the new ship with the old name, whose towering bulk rose before us. The side of the ship curved away from us and we could not see the stern. Above us, on the flight deck, we could see feet sticking out over the edge. The ship was painted grey and black, above and below the water line respectively. It did not seem as if she would be able to glide down to the River Mersey because she looked so tremendously heavy, but she had to play her to sea, the Band of the Royal Marines, who also played for the choir.

Then a sudden burst of cheering broke out, the cameramen moved into position and the crowd cheered and counter-cheered as Her Majesty the Queen walked on to the platform. She acknowledged the cheers and then the chief director of Camell Laird's showed her how to launch the "ARK". A short service was then held, conducted by Dr Crick. Then followed an expectant hush. The manager of Camell Laird's stepped forward and invited the Queen to launch the "ARK". She stepped forward, said a few words, lifted the traditional lead-covered bottle of champagne, let it drop and – crash! the bottle split, the champagne gushed out and slowly, very slowly, the boat began to move. Then it quickened and want yet faster, gliding along until it slid, with a slight spray, into its home river while the band played "Rule Britannia" and then, after a five minutes wait, the crowd began to disperse.

There have been three "ARK ROYALS". The first was built at Deptford for Sir Walter Raleigh. He christened her the "ARK" and after that the name of the owner, so she was called the "ARK RALEIGH". However, before her launching in 1587, she was taken over by the Government to fight the Armada and was re-christened "ARK ROYAL". She cost £5,000 and had nearly the displacement of a modern destroyer, 1,500 tons. She became the flagship of Lord Howard of Effingham, Lord High Admiral of England, and took a leading part in the destruction of the Armada. Later she was rebuilt and renamed, by James I, "Anne Royal" in honour of his wife and served as a flagship until wrecked in 1636. The second "ARK ROYAL" was the name applied in 1914, to the first large seaplane carrier, a converted merchant vessel which served in the Gallipoli campaign. Then, in 1935, when the Admiralty decided to build the third "ARK ROYAL", the old one was renamed "Pegasus" and was used for experimental aircraft work. The third "ARK ROYAL" cost £2,330,000, was 800 feet long and 94 feet wide. She carried 1,575 men and 60 aircraft. She was a member of Force H, the famous Mediterranean squadron which included the "ARK", "HOOD", "RENOWN", "SHEFFIELD" and "MALAYA". She helped in destroying the Bismarck and the Scharnhorst, covered landings and retreats, protected convoys, and hunted the Graf Spee. Then she was sunk in sight of Gibraltar by a torpedo attack with the loss of only one life. J N SHOBBROOK, IVa

The above has been reprinted verbatim from the Summer Term 1950 edition of The Inkwell. Shobbrook was a fourth-former and probably fourteen or fifteen years of age when he wrote it.

The Dr Crick referred to was the Lord Bishop of Chester and he was officiating there as Camell Laird's Shipyard at Birkenhead is in the Chester diocese.

The Ark Royal that was launched in 1950 was finally paid off in 1978 and broken up in 1980. The present Ark Royal was launched in 1978 and continues to serve.

CHAPTER TEN

Reserve Fleet

I was due to be demobbed on 23 November 1950 but the Korean War had started by then, and I can still hear Mr Clement Attlee's voice on the radio in October 1950 telling all National Servicemen that they were doing a fine job and would be required to serve an extra six months. I was already counting the days to my demobilisation, and had ordered a new suit ready for Civvy Street. I have a clear memory that a little earlier (in August 1950) the regular forces got an increase in pay, which did not apply to National Servicemen. A case of blatant discrimination.

The Royal Navy knew originally that they were going to lose my valuable services on 23 November, so I was drafted back to Devonport Barracks on 6 November. With my service being extended they then had the problem of what to do with me. I finished my time on HMS Howe, a battleship at anchor in the Tamar, where I served from 20 November 1950 to 15 May 1951. On that day I caught the 1315 boat to JAGO's and had to go through the usual joining routing. On Monday 21 May I had a final medical as part of the discharge routine. I was demobbed on 22 May 1951. We were let loose at 1400 and I caught the 1545 train. I must have got home late because on Wednesday 23 May I slept till noon. That's how I started my first day of freedom.

My posting to the Reserve Fleet was a total waste of time. HMS Howe was a floating barracks to accommodate surplus bodies from the main depot at Devonport. It was my first (and only) experience of an elaborate Job Creation Scheme. I remember little of my duties there, but they must have been performed satisfactorily, as they earned a glowing report from Lt Cdr (S) G W Protheroe on my History Sheet and promotion to Leading Stores Assistant (Victualling) on 28 February 1951. With this would go a welcome increase in pay, possibly to six shillings a day from four shillings. The highlight of the day was a very enjoyable cribbage school after lunch. Most afternoons at about 4 o'clock I would board the Liberty Boat, an MFV (Motor Fishing Vessel) to spend the evening in Plymouth, returning no later than 2359. I would normally be free at the week-ends provided I returned to ship by 0730 on Monday.

I should mention that not only were existing National Servicemen retained for an extra six months, but many ex-regulars who were on the Reserve List were recalled to the Colours. These were men who had signed on to do seven and five: seven years as regulars and five as reserves as an alternative to the more usual twelve years as a regular. I felt particularly sorry for Ed Curran, a Reservist from Newport in South Wales. He had qualified as a school teacher and was married. I met him on HMS Howe and he had even less work to do than me. It was criminal to drag him back from his new career when there was nothing for him to do. We became good friends. He always went home to Newport at the week-end but I never tried to make the long rail journey up to Chester. Every Friday Ed would ask me if I could lend him a pound or a couple of pounds for the railfare home. Lending money to shipmates was not something I would normally do but Ed always came up to me first thing on Monday morning and repaid me what I had lent him.

I had some sympathy also for a fellow National Serviceman, Roberts or Davies from Wrexham who was doing the extra six months. He had a job which would have been of particular value when he got demobbed – he was the assistant verger at St Nicholas' Church in the Barracks.

I learnt a very valuable lesson from one of the seamen on board. A lot of my messmates "followed the horses" and got their information from the Daily Mirror and suchlike. They would have a modest flutter on four or five races each day, and soon learned how difficult it was to beat the bookies. One member of the crew had a very different system, and one which frequently did mean beating the bookies. He had a brother or a cousin who worked in racing stables in Yorkshire and about once a month there would be a message that XYZ was running on Saturday in the 2.30 at Doncaster. He would then place a decent sized bet at attractive odds with a Plymouth bookmaker, and seven or eight times out of ten he would be successful. He never mentioned the name of the horse until after the race as otherwise the bookmakers in Plymouth would have been besieged with dozens of sailors all trying to get on the same certainty, and the odds would have shortened very quickly. So I learned the value of good inside information at an early age. I've never had a brother or a cousin working in a racing stable, so I have always kept a good distance from the bookies.

Once I had been posted to the Reserve Fleet I had much greater opportunity to go to concerts and football matches. On the Wizard we were on a four-week rota with the other ships in the flotilla – one week on duty, one week on standby and two weeks off-duty. But there would always be regular watch keeping duties which kept me on board. It was much easier once I was on board HMS Howe to go ashore.

In the 1940s Chester was very much a soccer city. Only a few public schoolboys played rugger in those days. All the local day schools were soccer schools. I discovered when I reached Plymouth that the South West was a Rugby Union stronghold, and that Plymouth Albion and Devonport Services (the Royal Navy's own XV) were at least as important as Plymouth Argyle at Home Park. I went to quite a few rugby matches but never really got into it – the referee seemed to be blowing his whistle an awful lot and no one seemed to know what infringements were being penalised.

The Barbarians visited Plymouth whilst I was there and I also attended a memorable match at Home Park when Plymouth Argyle played Preston North End and the legendary Tom Finney turned out for the visitors.

It is clear from my diaries that I was a more regular and diligent churchgoer in those days. In fact, whilst I was hanging about in barracks waiting for a posting, I joined the choir of St Nicholas' Church, the splendid church actually inside HMS Drake. My membership was soon cut short because a couple of weeks later I was posted to HMS Wizard, and regular attendance at that church was out of the question.

When I was able to go into Plymouth on a Sunday evening I had a preference for St Andrew's Church, right in the centre of the city. The church had been badly damaged in the blitz and it was linked at that time with St Catherine's.

The Vicar of the combined churches was the Right Reverend Norman H Clarke MA, Bishop of Plymouth and he concluded his ministry at St Andrew's on Sunday 31 December 1950. He must have been a Suffrogan Bishop in the Exeter diocese.

After the evening service the Vicar invited those who wished to stay behind for a discussion group at the Vicarage. I was clearly ahead of my time in 1950, much more ecumenically minded than other members of the congregation.

The Rector was horrified when I attacked the divisions in the Christian Churches, and advocated a comprehensive amalgamation of the Anglicans, Roman Catholics and Free Churches. Some years later the Anglicans and Methodists held abortive talks about a possible union, and the Presbyterians and Congregationalists did amalgamate to form the United Reformed Church. After my outspoken (and clearly unwelcome) comments the Vicar looked at me in rather a different light. What an expert I must have been on these subjects at the ripe old age of nineteen.

It is interesting to me that there is a much more friendly and co-operative atmosphere these days between the various Christian Churches in most of the British Isles.

Not to be taken away till November 26

PARISH CHURCH OF

St. Andrew with St. Catherine
PLYMOUTH

Vicar :
Right Rev. Norman H. Clarke, M.A.
Bishop of Plymouth

November, 1950

The Introit (every Sunday before the 11 a.m. Service).
God is a spirit; they who worship Him in spirit and in truth must bow the knee. O Thou who dwellest mid the cherubim, draw nigh to us while we draw nigh to Thee.

CHAPTER ELEVEN

Youth Hostelling

Once aboard HMS Howe it was easier to get week-end leave, sometimes SWE, occasionally LWE (short week-end/long week-end). I calculated that it just wasn't worth making the long tedious train journey home to Chester so I decided to go Youth Hostelling in Devon and Cornwall. This involved a lot of hiking and hitchhiking. Hitchhiking was still a respectable and reputable activity in 1950 and very much a legacy from the war years when thumbing a lift was often the best way servicemen and women could get home quickly and cheaply. I stayed at Lownard on a few occasions, presumably because it was the nearest and most easily accessible Youth Hostel. Membership cards were always stamped and occasionally date-stamped and so I know that I also stayed at the Youth Hostels at Lostwithiel, Bigbury-on-Sea, Salcombe, Brentwater, Bellever and Pool Mill. The hostel I stayed at most frequently was Belmont in Plymouth itself. It had two main attractions. Firstly, as distinct from Aggie Westons and the YMCA, it was not frequented by other naval personnel; it was a completely civilian environment and that was attractive and important to me. Possibly of greater significance was that it had a grand piano which the warden allowed me to play. My 1951 diary records the various treks I made across the moors but these details are not interesting enough to be reprinted. There were, however, two diary entries which are worth including. On Saturday 10 February 1951 I stayed at Bigbury-on-Sea and after supper there was a grand log fire and an easy chair. I read Pamela Frankau's Manual of Manners. On Saturday 28 April 1951 I stayed at Bellever and recorded: Grand company Dartmoor Rambling Club Country dancing in dining room and roaring log fire in common room.

What simple pleasures! Normally there would not be many people staying in the hostels at that time of the year. But for me it was a few precious hours among civilians and young people and away from naval discipline and restrictions.

The atmosphere in the hostels was rather different from today. I have reprinted the Extracts from the Rules and Regulations and The Country Code. Nowadays people turn up by car and in coaches and the facilities have been modernised. The costs have also multiplied. I recollect that we paid one and sixpence (7.5 new pence) or one and ninepence (8.25 new pence) per night and probably about the same amount if we had an evening meal.

The Youth Hostel, Lownard

Youth Hostels Association
Extracts from Rules and Regulations
1. Youth Hostels are for the use of members who travel on foot, by bicycle or canoe; they are not for members touring by motor-car, motor-cycle or similar vehicle.
2. On arrival at a hostel:
   > Hand this card to the warden.
   > Pay the overnight charge.
   > Sign the housebook.
   > Make up your bed.

   In the event of any complaint against the member the warden may retain the membership card and his decision will stand pending an appeal to the Regional Group to which the member belongs.
3. A sheet sleeping bag of approved type must be used.
4. Hostels are closed between 10am and 5pm.
5. Members must be in the hostel by 10pm.
6. Members must do their share of hostel duties.
7. Intoxicants are not allowed in the hostels and smoking in the dormitories is prohibited.
8. Y.H.A. members have gained a reputation for sensible behaviour in the countryside. You can help to maintain that reputation and encourage others to do likewise. Wanton damage is not likely to be caused by hostellers, but little thoughtless actions committed by many people may create a serious nuisance. Therefore, for the good name of the Y.H.A., you are asked to respect the privacy and property of local residents and to keep in mind the Country Code printed inside this card.

The Country Code
Avoid damaging crops (including mowing-grass) in any way.

Do not disturb cattle or sheep. Keep dogs always under control.

Protect crops, plantations, ricks, etc, against fire. Don't drop lighted matches or cigarette ends.

Close all gates, unless they are obviously intended to be left open.

Be careful not to damage trees, hedges, fences or walls.

Clear up all your litter, including glass.

Be specially careful never to foul pools or streams.

Pick wild flowers sparingly, if at all, and never dig them up.

Do not rob birds' nests.

Enjoy the countryside, but do not hinder the work of the countryman.

Buckfast Abbey

TWELVE

Chester Arts Week 1950

Apart from Youth Hostelling my other great interest and pleasure was classical music. I must make a brief reference to this as I was very surprised to make a discovery about an Arts Week in 1950 among my old papers. Chester now has a very successful well-established Summer Music Festival each year. If you were to ask any of the people attending the concerts about the origin of the Festival the name of Martin Merry would crop up. Mr Merry was the Director of Music at the King's School and was the driving force behind the Summer Music Festival in its early days in the 1970's. There was also a marvellous Arts Festival in 1967 (some time before Martin Merry) when Paul Tortelier and his family came to Chester while the Mystery Plays were being performed and there was one unforgettable afternoon in the Town Hall when all four members of the family gave a recital. Madame Maud Martin Tortelier was also a cellist, Yan Pascal a violinist and Maria de la Pau (the daughter) a pianist. The programme told us inter alia that Yan Pascal had won the first prize at the Paris Conservatoire in 1961 and that Maria de la Pau was a god daughter of Casals. The artistic directors of the Arts Festival were Peter Dornford May and John Sanders and the administrator was David Laing. I was surprised to discover that I must have had at a long week-end at home in October 1950, possibly to get a new suit ready for when I was demobbed. The Arts Week from 1 to 7 October was presented by Chester City Council following a very

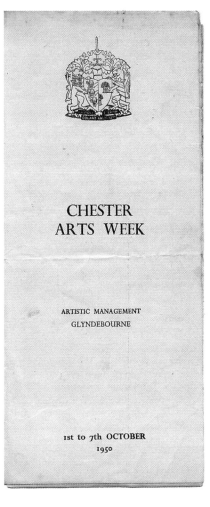

CHESTER ARTS WEEK

ARTISTIC MANAGEMENT
GLYNDEBOURNE

1st to 7th OCTOBER
1950

successful Civic Arts Week in 1949. The centrepiece of the Arts Week were performances at the Gaumont Theatre by the London Opera Society. The whole event was under the artistic management of Glyndebourne. I remember feeling that the choice of operas left a lot to be desired:- The Night Bell by Donizetti, Le Pauvre Matelot by Milhaud, The Secret Marriage by Cimarosa.
I don't think that Chester was ready, in 1950, for such a choice of unusual operas. I am sure that the repertoire of the Carl Rosa Opera Company would have been more attractive for most people.

CHAPTER THIRTEEN

Civvy Street

The first day after I was demobbed – 23 May 1951 – must have been the happiest day of my life up to that point. I couldn't wait to get back to my old job and to resume my apprenticeship. I went to see my old boss on Friday 25 May to tell him that I was home, and I was back at my desk on Monday 28 May. I had to go to the Food Office to get a Ration Book and Clothing Coupons and probably the Labour Exchange to get a National Health Insurance card.

Many other National Servicemen felt as I did. We had been conscripted to serve our King and Country; most of us had left comfortable, secure homes and had had our careers interrupted. We had exchanged a pleasant life at home for a pretty hard existence and a lot of discomfort for a miserable four shillings a day. While we were doing our National Service, however, we were the envy of many of our shipmates who had signed on for long-service engagements and were now regretting it.

As we were peace-time conscripts we didn't qualify for a medal, a gratuity or a demob suit. We didn't even get a letter of thanks or appreciation – just a rather cold instruction, warning us to keep our uniforms in good order, or else!

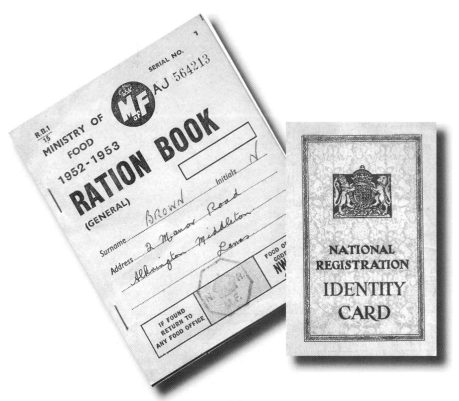

What sort of a world were we returning to when we got demobbed in 1951? Certainly vastly different from today. Homelife and family ties were stronger in the Fifties. There was more visiting to and from relatives. We would sit down for more meals together, and particularly Sunday lunch was a recognised family occasion. I am genuinely surprised to read in my diaries the names of those who sent me letters when I was in the Royal Navy and to whom, of course, I sent replies. Grandparents, aunts and uncles, great aunts and great uncles, brother and sisters, cousins, old school friends, colleagues at work. There was no television and the radio and gramophone records were important for music in the home. Long before tapes and compact discs and walkmans. The cinema and the theatre were the main outside entertainments until the advent of television.

I lived in a street of about fifty terraced houses, and not one person in our street owned a car. I don't think that anybody had a telephone. We all had to use the kiosk at the end of the road. Not one child in my junior class at school came by car. And most of us went home after school without our mothers meeting us.

Wages were low, as were rents, house prices and mortgage repayments. The cost of living was very stable; index-linking was very much in the future. We tended to have most of our meals at home; eating out had not become a fashion, and few pubs, if any, provided bar snacks or meals. We had shorter holidays and longer working hours. Most people worked on Saturday mornings; the five-day week came in later. Many people got just one week's paid annual holiday, but two weeks was not uncommon. Anyone who got three weeks in those days probably qualified for it by serving their firm for twenty years. Holidays abroad were not possible during the war years and all my holidays were spent staying with relatives. Bank Holidays were more important. Most towns and cities had a regular Early-Closing Day (usually a Wednesday or a Thursday) and all the shops in the area abided by this.

Support for local football clubs and cricket clubs was stronger. Most people who went to see my local football team (Third Division – North) either went on foot, by bicycle or on the special football buses run by the Corporation Transport Department. Once people got their own cars they could start going to Manchester and Liverpool to see the First Division teams. Cheshire is not a strong cricket county, but we read with interest of the matches in the Lancashire League and their star professionals (one per team). The names of Learie Constantine and Cec Pepper come to mind.

It seemed to be a much safer country in the 1950s. I don't recall defenceless little old ladies being mugged in the streets.

There were no discos blaring out their noise into the early hours of the morning. Dancehalls closed at midnight and it was safe for young girls to walk home. The divorce rate was still low, one-parent families had not become commonplace, teachers were not in fear of being attacked by their pupils or the parents and the idea of having police patrols inside schools would have been ludicrous. The word "drugs" was never mentioned. We were a more law-abiding society and everybody felt much safer in those days.

There was plenty of work for everybody. The words unemployment and redundancy were never mentioned. There was full employment, probably overfull employment. Industrial Tribunals and claims for unfair dismissal were unheard of.

My own office was typical of professional offices throughout the country. Some things were almost Dickensian; very little had changed since the Twenties and Thirties.

I remember when the first ballpoint pens (biros) arrived. We had long earnest discussions as to whether cheques could be signed with these newfangled pens. For a long time people continued to sign cheques, letters and documents with pen and ink, often a Parker fountain pen. So blotting paper was in regular use. Is there an office anywhere in the country which still uses blotting paper? If you wanted a lot of copies of anything there was the Gestetner, Ellams or Roneo rotary duplicator. The typists had to prepare a special skin and often got black blotches on their clothes from the ink in the machine. Photocopiers arrived much later. Most of the bookkeeping was manual; Kalamazoo was a popular system at the time. The more advanced firms were starting to install machine accounting for their ledgers, and the really go-ahead ones had punched card systems (Hollerith or Powers Samas). Most of the additions had to be checked in our heads, but we did have a comptometer operator for the bigger audits. Sellotape had not been invented and when I posted a parcel of books back to a client a candle was lit and shiny red sealing wax was put on all the knots. Pocket calculators, electric typewriters, postal franking machines, shredding machines and of course word processors and computers were all a long way ahead in the future.

We hadn't got much money and there was not a lot to spend it on. Furniture and clothes were not very stylish, and still had the wartime utility mark on them. The New Look in fashion was yet to come. Hire purchase was in its infancy and people tended to save up first if they wanted to buy anything. Credit cards were a thing for the future.I imagine that my life after I was demobbed was similar to many of my National Service comrades. I finished my apprenticeship, passed my professional exams, worked for a couple of years for a big firm in London, got married, started a family, moved house two or three times as the family grew bigger, and climbed the ladder at work. My memories of my "happy days" in the Royal Navy faded pretty quickly. But I was always very proud of having served in the Royal Navy and I was invited more than once to join the Chester branch of the RNA Club. I never felt at ease socialising with a bunch of old salts who could reminisce for hours about their postings to Malta, Trincomalee, the West Indies and other exotic places. I am not against ex-servicemens organisations. They fulfil a need and perform a useful service. I just didn't feel properly qualified to join.

Balancing the books with Harry Thomason. Old Bank Buildings, Chester, 1953

I never cease to marvel at the Obituary page of the Daily Telegraph – their archives about retired generals, admirals and air marshals must be wondrous to behold. I always glance through the life stories of retired admirals and other senior naval personnel to see which ships they served in. Not once in twenty or thirty years have I ever seen any reference to HMS Wizard.

I realise now that the Wizard had a rather undistinguished record in the Second World War. The Wizard was a W (Wager) class destroyer built by Vickers Armstrong at Barrow-in-Furness and went into service on 30 March 1944. In May 1944 she was engaged in the aircraft carrier raids against Norwegian shipping regions, but in the following month Wizard was badly damaged by an explosion of her own depth charges. The extensive repairs took until April 1945 and this is why she saw so little action against the German navy. After VE day she was despatched to join the British Pacific Fleet, and was one of the ships in Tokyo Bay for the acceptance of the Japanese surrender in September 1945. She returned to the United Kingdom via New Zealand and Australia and joined Plymouth Command in 1946. Her captain commanded the Plymouth Flotilla which was employed on routine duties and special trials until January 1952 when the Wizard was withdrawn from service for conversion into a Type 15 anti-submarine frigate.

I used to glance occasionally at the small advertisement section of such magazines as The Lady, the Saga Magazine, the WI Magazine (Home & Country) which include dates for reunions of schools, army units, airforce squadrons and ships. Never once have I seen any mention of a reunion for the ratings of HMS Wizard.

Imagine my astonishment therefore when I opened my Daily Telegraph towards the end of August 1982, to learn that Rear-Admiral Derek Reffell had taken over command of the naval task force for the Falklands from Rear-Admiral Sandy Woodward in June, and that his flagship was HMS Bristol a Type 82 Destroyer of 6,750 tons.

CHAPTER FOURTEEN

Annus Mirabilis

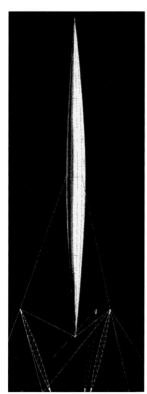

Looking back to 1951, when I returned to Civvy Street, I now wonder if I was right to feel that National Service had been rather a waste of time. I am sure that I was not alone in this feeling but I knew that I had been luckier than most. For the first eighteen months of my service I had been extremely busy, and it was only after Mr Attlee's radio announcement that the time dragged and became rather pointless. Many National Servicemen had had boring jobs and felt that the whole of their two years' service had been a waste of time.

As one who is now a lot older, and hopefully, a little wiser. I think on reflection that 1950 was possibly one of the most challenging and interesting years of my life.

I had joined up in May 1949 and spent the first six months undergoing training, and with virtually no "hands on" practical experience. In November 1949 I was posted to a destroyer with sole responsibility for maintaining food supplies on board. I was really "on my own", as my superior the Coxswain, a senior Chief Petty Officer with many other duties, was only too happy to leave Victualling matters to me,

The Skylon - symbol of the provided that nothing went wrong. I was 19 years of age, had
Festival of Britain, 1951 my own little office and plenty of work to do. Thinking back I am surprised that the "powers that be" in Devonport should have placed all this responsibility on my young, inexperienced shoulders. But they gave me a great opportunity to show what I could do.

Why do I now regard 1950 as such a marvellous year? Apart from an interesting, responsible job I think of all the different people I met – Officers, Chief Petty Officers, Petty Officers, Leading Hands and other ratings. I think also of the interesting places we visited, largely of course through the Summer Programme – Guernsey, Ilfracombe, Milford Haven, Cardiff, Paignton, Torquay, Dartmouth, Dover and Cherbourg. I had also had a memorable holiday in France. When we were not on duty or on standby I went into Devonport and Plymouth most evenings and weekends. Plymouth was a bigger city than Chester and had better plays, operas and concerts. It had been badly bombed during the war and there was very little left standing in the middle. The city fathers had laid down the main roads across this waste land – one was called Armada Way. St Andrew's Church had been severely damaged, but there did not seem to be too much harm to the large houses on the hill going up to the Hoe. What a wonderful open space that is, looking out to the breakwater and Drake's Island. It is a glorious spot. Union Street with its pubs and the Palace Theatre seemed to have escaped the worst of the bombing. My main ports of call were the NAAFI, the YMCA, Agnes Westons Sailors' Home and the Youth Hostel, usually to try to get a decent meal.

I was a regular user of the small music room at the NAAFI. This was in the days before LPs and they had a modest selection of the old 78s of popular classical music. Standing out among the rather hackneyed favourites they had a recording of Elgar's Symphony No 2, a work I had never heard before. It is not the easiest of symphonies at the first hearing, but I played it so many times that it became, for a while, my favourite symphony, and I am still very fond of it despite it being rarely played these days.

Before I was called up I had been an active member of the Youth Hostels Association and very often when I had weekend leave I would stay at the Youth Hostels in Devon and Cornwall. I had money in my pocket (not very much at four shillings a day) and I was determined to see the world. 1950 must have been a wonderful year, although it may not have seemed so at the time.

I had joined the Royal Navy in May 1949 as a quiet, reserved youth from a secure and sheltered family background. When I returned home in May 1951 I was a more confident young man. The main legacy of my two years in the Royal Navy was that I had learnt a lot about people and human nature and how to look after myself. I had more self-esteem and more self-assurance. In modern parlance I was definitely more streetwise.

1950 was just another of those drab, grey early post-war years. Food and clothes rationing were still in force. Things started to brighten up with the Festival of Britain in 1951. That was quickly followed by the unexpected death of King George VI, the accession of his daughter as Queen Elizabeth II and the Coronation in 1953 and the conquest of Everest by Hillary and Tensing.

In retrospect the Festival of Britain of 1951 was an important event marking the transition from the war and its hardships and shortages and the hopes for our peacetime future. It commemorated also the centenary of one of the greatest events of the Victorian Age, the Great Exhibition of 1851. People were ready for something novel and inspiring and the Festival captured the public's imagination. Visitors poured into London to go to the South Bank. The Royal Festival Hall has been a magnificent legacy and a great asset to the capital for over fifty years. It only heightens ones sense of disappointment at the mismanagement of the Millennium celebrations in 2000 and the ludicrous Dome built at vast public expense, and now an embarrassing white elephant. What was happening in 1950 in the world at large? A recent Christmas gift was a book CENTURY published by Phaidon, one hundred years of Human Progress, Regression, Suffering and Hope conceived and edited by Bruce Bernard. Mr Bernard's selection of photographs for 1950 is dominated by the now largely forgotten and rarely mentioned Korean War, but there are a handful of interesting intruders:-

- Henri Matisse at work in his studio. He carried on working until his death at the age of 85 in 1954.
- Billy Graham addressing a vast crowd in London.
- Jackson Pollock, the American artist, at work. Pollock died in 1956 at the age of 44.
- Chaim Weizmann the first President of Israel, casting his vote in the municipal elections. Weizmann died in 1952.
- Togliatti, the Italian Communist leader in hospital after a car accident. Togliatti died in 1964.
- Betty Hutton playing Annie Oakley in the film version of Annie Get Your Gun.

CHAPTER FIFTEEN

Loose Ends

One of the first things I did when I got demobbed was to buy myself a piano. The family instrument was well past its "sell by" date and it needed to be replaced. There were no new pianos available in 1951 as all production of luxury goods had been halted at the start of the Second World War. Even if new goods were obtainable they carried a hefty rate of purchase tax, so there was a flourishing market in second-hand, reconditioned musical instruments and items such as jewellery. I had for a long time admired a friend's beautiful Rogers upright piano and decided to buy a similar one if I could. Rogers showroom was in Duke Street, off Grosvenor Square in London and I went down on the train one Saturday morning. The showroom was due to close at 1 o'clock and I arrived at about 12.30pm to have a look at the three second-hand pianos within my price range. I had to make a quick decision. I still have the invoice dated 21 July 1951 for that wonderful piano. I cannot understand how I came to have £142-2-6 in July 1951. I had had four shillings a day for most of my national service, increased to six shillings a day for the final few months. When I resumed work at my office my initial salary was the princely sum of two pounds per week. I just cannot work out how I amassed nearly £150 to buy a superb piano. It was probably the best purchase I have ever made. I kept the old Rogers until 1988 when I had the chance to acquire an equally beautiful John Broadwood boudoir grand. When I finally parted with the Rogers I sold it for two or three times the amount I had paid for it in 1951.

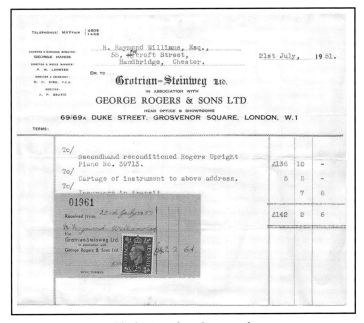

The best purchase I ever made

I was very much a civilian again when a letter arrived on Saturday 8 March 1952 from Royal Naval Special Reserve in Devonport. This told me that I would be required to report for my annual training in June, so I had to tell my boss straightaway to arrange leave of absence from the office. In due course I received a one-way rail warrant to Weymouth so that I could join the aircraft carrier HMS Indefatigable moored at Portland. The only thing I remember about Weymouth is that I went to the Variety Show at the Ritz Theatre where none other than Max Miller, in his outrageous flashy suit, was top of the bill. The fortnight's training for the Special Reservists was almost like a cruise ship holiday. The officers and crew of the aircraft carrier had no idea what to do with us. We were a total embarrassment to them.

I knew a few of the other Reservists and it was a most enjoyable reunion. We sailed up the English Channel towards Dover and then sailed northwards along the east coast of England and Scotland until we reached Invergordon, north of Inverness. There I was given a one-way rail warrant from Dingwall to Chester. The journey home probably took all day, but I had had a buckshee holiday at the government's expense. I had enjoyed it so much that in 1953 when I didn't hear anything from RNSR at Devonport I wrote and asked them if they could let me know when I would be needed as I wanted to plan a youth hostelling holiday in Austria. I was disappointed to hear that my services would not be required in 1953, and I never got a call for any of the later years.

Possibly that was just as well if I had had to take my uniform with me. It was becoming less and less intact. The Action Working Dress (No 8s) was particularly useful for wearing in the garden and for household repair jobs. Later on my peaked caps were very popular with my children and their friends for playing bus conductors and train drivers.

H.M.S. INDEFATIGABLE

presents:

. June Revue .

At Portland

11th & 12th June, 1952

•

By kind permission of
Captain J. W. Grant, D.S.O., Royal Navy

8. MARTYN and COOKE
   A Juggling Cocktail

9. MARTIN CROSBIE and THELMA
   The Popular Irish Singer

10. THE ONE AND ONLY
    MAX MILLER

11. FINALE

Weymouth 1952

41

And what of HMS Wizard itself? After conversion to a Type 15 fast anti-submarine frigate in 1954, Wizard returned to Plymouth to join the 3rd Training Squadron and remained in service until 1965, when she was paid off and placed on the disposal list. She was eventually sold for breaking up in 1967 and was finally broken up at Inverkeithing in July 1971.

And finally a word of thanks and appreciation to the Youth Hostels Association. It had been the source of immense pleasure in the three years 1946, 1947 and 1948 before I joined the Royal Navy. Whilst I was doing my National Service I was glad to be able to stay at their hostels (including a memorable holiday in France). When I got back to Civvy Street in 1951 I resumed my membership of the YHA and joined their Club in Chester which had weekly meetings for local enthusiasts. This group prospered to such an extent that they started a weekly Scottish Country Dance at a rather scruffy church hall in a run down part of the city. It was more of a class than a dance. I can still see Margot clapping her hands and imploring us to take our partners and to get into line. She would have done well in the ATS. The more serious dancers acquired those rather attractive dancing shoes, but I, in company with many others, never rose above a pair of plimsolls. I started going to St Barnabas (Barnies) fairly regularly on Friday evenings in October 1953 and soon met a very attractive young lady from Manchester who was working in one of our Chester hospitals. It took me many months before I plucked up the courage to ask her for a date and this was almost a disaster.

The cricket club were having their end of season dance on Friday 24 September 1954 and I needed a partner as I didn't have a girlfriend at that time. I was pleasantly surprised to receive a positive answer when I invited this attractive young lady from Manchester to come

HMS Wizard off Dover 1950

to the cricket club dance. I was quite convinced that she would say no. I then did rather a clever thing. I was a bit worried about the cricket club dance – would it be a howling success or a gigantic flop? It could so easily be either. So I booked two tickets for the Liverpool Philharmonic Orchestra for the following Saturday evening (to be conducted by Sir Thomas Beecham) and asked my dance partner if she would be interested in going. I also managed to persuade her to come with me to Goodison Park in the afternoon to see Everton draw with Cardiff City 1-1. The day out in Liverpool rescued me after the complete fiasco of the cricket club dance. We got engaged in 1955 and Miss Brown became Mrs Williams on 11 August 1956. And that's a totally different and wonderful story.

A very attractive young lady from Manchester 1955

I used to see from time to time letters to the editor advocating the return of National Service. I haven't seen any such letters for quite some time, but perhaps the subject might surface again. I have been very forthright about conscription being regarded as a waste of time, but these views are from a very personal, and possibly selfish, point of view. I appreciate now that, apart from the outbreak of the Korean War in June 1950, we had the Russian blockade of Berlin and the airlift of supplies to that city starting in July 1948 – and lasting until September 1949. We had fallen out with our wartime ally rather quickly and the Cold War was to continue for over forty years. The Soviet bloc maintained massive armed forces and we dare not run down our own defence capability.

National Service eventually ended in 1960. The service chiefs would obviously prefer a smaller highly-trained, fully professional fighting force than one made up largely of unenthusiastic short term conscripts. It's different with the TA and the RNVR because they are volunteers who are keen to get involved and they provide a valuable additional force. National Service was probably not a cost-effective way of strengthening our defences, and the more so with the huge advances in technology.

CHAPTER SIXTEEN

Sex and Violence

You will have realised long ago that this was not some raunchy bodice-ripper aimed at the great British reading public. The received wisdom is that a book needs its fair share of sex and violence to ensure commercial success. So let me do what I can to follow the crowd. I didn't have a regular girlfriend when I was called up in 1949. Outside of work my main interest in those days was playing football and cricket, and a girlfriend would get in the way of this. Also we had no money, and girlfriends cost money! I was however on friendly terms with a lot of girls, the typists at the office, the members of the Youth Fellowship and my sisters' school friends who were often at our house.

I was only at Corsham for four weeks and at Wetherby for three months and I doubt if the local girls would take much interest in any of us, despite our smart naval uniforms. Plymouth was different as it was a garrison city of thousands of young men and a few hundred young women, so the girls could take their pick. They were unlikely to be interested in National Servicemen on four shillings a day. Also the sort of girls I might have been interested in – eighteen or nineteen year old ex-grammar school types were probably away at university or training college. Had they been at home in Plymouth I am certain that they would have been much keener on the local boys who were not going to disappear after a few weeks or months.

I don't remember having any meaningful contact with the Wrens. In my mind's eye I imagine them all as being very attractive and nice looking rather like the early air stewardesses. The Wrens had their Wrennery at St Budeaux, a mile or two up the road from Naval Barracks and they probably went ashore (into town) in their civvies rather than in their uniforms. Here again the Wrens would be outnumbered fifty to one, or a hundred to one so they could definitely pick and choose. I am certain they all had very full engagement diaries, and that not many of them went out with National Servicemen.

Prior to 1949 I doubt if I had any very clear ideas about homosexuality. I remember that we once had a Latin master at school who was rather effeminate, but it did not raise too many eyebrows. In Devonport it was slightly unnerving to see a couple of ratings from the Wizard cavorting round the streets in blonde wigs with heavily made up faces in slinky dresses, nylons and highheeled shoes and carrying handbags! There were only two transvestites out of a ship's company of two hundred and they were despised or pitied by the others as a pathetic joke. They would inevitably attract some pretty crude and ribald comments as well from the more uncouth members of the ship's company. Political correctness had not yet come in.

Violence is very easily dealt with – virtually nothing to report!

I can visualise very clearly the Naval patrols in their distinctive white gaiters marching in twos along Union Street. From time to time, on Saturday nights, some of the lads would have had too much scrumpy and there were occasional brawls at closing time outside the public houses. The civil police would be happy to leave these disturbances to the naval police, and all those apprehended would be up before the Captain early on Monday morning. The justice administered probably fell short of European Human Rights legislation, but it was inexpensive, prompt, impartial, decisive, severe and effective. The maintenance of good order and discipline was always the foremost consideration.

45

Acknowledgements and Thanks

- Eileen McCarthy for her artistic skill with the illustrations, and for setting out the text, prior to publication by her company 4 Corners Publishing.

- Kendall Press Manchester for printing and binding the book

- Admiral Sir Derek Reffell for contributing the foreword to the book

- John Shobbrook for so readily agreeing to the inclusion of his schoolboy article about H.M.S. Ark Royal

- Gordan Emery, the Chester author and publisher, for his professional advice and help at the proof-reading stage

- Elizabeth Wakley of Bookland in Chester, and Jennifer Minchin of University Bookseller in Plymouth for undertaking the retail distribution